SYDNEY 2013
THE CITY AT A GLANCE

Mrs Macquaries Point
Gaze out over the world-famous harbour
from one of the best 'seats' in the city – a
chair carved into the sandstone peninsula.
Mrs Macquaries Road

Art Gallery of New South Wales
Exhibited here is one of the
permanent collections of
Torres Strait Islander art i
Art Gallery Road, T 9225 17

Sydney Tower
From the 268m observatic
city's telecoms mast you'll
amazing views of the Blue
the west and Botany Bay to
100 Market Street

Government House
This Gothic revival mansion is the residence
of the governor of New South Wales. It is
open to visitors from Friday to Sunday.
Macquarie Street, T 9931 5222

Governor Phillip Tower
Denton Corker Marshall's skyscraper was
completed in 1993, and is most notable
for the epic proportions of its skylit foyer.
Phillip/Bridge Street

Sydney Opera House
The sails of Jørn Utzon's masterwork are said
to have been inspired by segments of orange.
He left the project after a row in 1966, but
returned to it in 1999 to design an extension.
See p014

The Rocks
Sydney's historic core has some of the city's
oldest buildings. It was home to the Gadigal
people before the Europeans arrived in 1788.

INTRODUCTION
THE CHANGING FACE OF THE URBAN SCENE

It's all about that harbour. Regardless of the manmade landmarks so synonymous with Sydney, the Opera House and the Harbour Bridge, its natural beauty is jaw-dropping. Fringed by exquisite bays and beaches, and dotted with islands, it is both postcard and playground – if you've ever seen the New Year's Eve celebrations, from flotilla to fireworks, you'll know what we mean. To get your bearings, take a ferry to Manly Beach on the North Shore for a swim in the surf and a beachside beer against a backdrop of pines.

It's easy to be seduced by the scenery, but the city has far more going for it than its looks. It is incredibly easy to have fun here. Known for its high-end cuisine and rowdy pubs and clubs, Sydney has developed a deeper level of sophistication as independent bars and boutiques have flourished. This scene is to the fore in the fashion and foodie enclaves of Surry Hills and Darlinghurst, in Balmain – an arty harbourside haven – and in the urban grunge of Newtown. The globalisation of Sydneysiders continues apace; about 200 nationalities are now represented in the city and its surrounds, and districts such as Haberfield, Petersham and Cabramatta are rich in Italian, Portuguese and Vietnamese flavour.

Thanks to the added attraction of year-round sunshine, Sydney puts on some of the country's biggest artistic and cultural events, from the Mardi Gras parade to Vivid Sydney, a festival of light and music. It's little wonder so many come to visit and never leave.

ESSENTIAL INFO

FACTS, FIGURES AND USEFUL ADDRESSES

TOURIST OFFICE
Sydney Visitor Centre
Argyle/Playfair Street
T 9240 8788
www.sydneyvisitorcentre.com

TRANSPORT
Buses
T 131 500
www.sydneybuses.info
Car hire
Avis
395 Pitt Street
T 8255 1616
CityRail
T 131 500
www.cityrail.info
Trains run from 4.30am to 1am, Monday
to Friday; 5.30am to 1am at weekends
Taxis
Silver Service
T 133 100

EMERGENCY SERVICES
Emergencies
T 000
Police (non-emergencies)
T 9265 6499
Late-night pharmacy
Blake's Pharmacy
20 Darlinghurst Road
T 9358 6712

CONSULATES
British Consulate-General
1 Macquarie Place
T 9247 7521
www.ukinaustralia.fco.gov.uk
US Consulate-General
19-29 Martin Place
T 9373 9200
sydney.usconsulate.gov

POSTAL SERVICES
Post office
1 Martin Place
T 131 318
Shipping
UPS
T 131 877
www.ups.com

BOOKS
**Radical Sydney: Places, Portraits
and Unruly Episodes** by Terry Irving
and Rowan Cahill (UNSW Press)
Sydney Opera House: Jørn Utzon by
Philip Drew (Phaidon)

WEBSITES
Design
www.object.com.au
www.visualarts.net.au
Newspapers
www.theaustralian.com.au
www.smh.com.au

EVENTS
Sydney Festival
www.sydneyfestival.org.au
Mardi Gras
www.mardigras.org.au

COST OF LIVING
**Taxi from Kingsford Smith
airport to city centre**
A$45
Cappuccino
A$3.50
Packet of cigarettes
A$15
Daily newspaper
A$1.70
Bottle of champagne
A$80

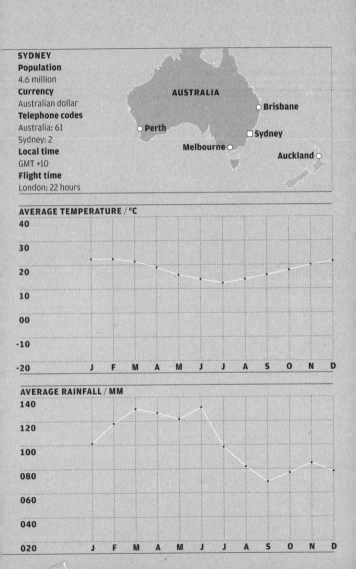

SYDNEY
Population
4.6 million
Currency
Australian dollar
Telephone codes
Australia: 61
Sydney: 2
Local time
GMT +10
Flight time
London: 22 hours

AUSTRALIA

Brisbane

Perth

Sydney

Melbourne

Auckland

AVERAGE TEMPERATURE / °C

| | J | F | M | A | M | J | J | A | S | O | N | D |
40
30
20
10
00
-10
-20

AVERAGE RAINFALL / MM

140
120
100
080
060
040
020

| | J | F | M | A | M | J | J | A | S | O | N | D |

NEIGHBOURHOODS
THE AREAS YOU NEED TO KNOW AND WHY

To help you navigate the city, we've chosen the most interesting districts (see below and the map inside the back cover) and colour-coded our featured venues, according to their location; those venues that are outside these areas are not coloured.

BONDI

Sydney's celebrated beach isn't nearly as beautiful as those found to the north of the city, but it is *the* destination for visitors and Sydneysiders alike when a fix of sand, surf and refreshments is in order. Call in at the casual North Bondi Italian Food (see p050) for a post-swim cocktail and clam linguine. It is worth noting that the folk who live in Bondi tend to gather exclusively at the north end of the beach.

DARLINGHURST/SURRY HILLS

Among the most diverse of Sydney's centrally located neighbourhoods is the bohemian-meets-trendsetting pairing of Surry Hills and Darlinghurst. This part of the city has everything – fantastic shopping (see p080), fine dining (see p044) and people-watching – and it is home to the city's gay community. Much of the area is in the process of being revamped, including the dowdy part of Oxford Street that runs through here.

WATERLOO

This suburb, situated to the south of the city centre, is definitely on the rise. In recent years there has been an influx of residents in many of the area's newly built apartment blocks, as well as independent retailers who find the high rents within the more established areas suffocating. If you have a little time, walk around the neighbourhood and explore the art galleries, shops and cafés on Danks Street.

POTTS POINT/KINGS CROSS

There's action 24 hours a day in Kings Cross. Once the red-light district, this area is being gradually cleaned up, due largely to community campaigning. Walk down Darlinghurst Road, which morphs into Macleay Street, and you will find yourself in a much more genteel part of town, Potts Point, where the streets are lined with cafés, restaurants (see p048), stores and glorious 1930s apartment blocks.

PADDINGTON

Oxford Street's eastern end has been hit hard by the economic downturn, but the backstreets harbour excellent art galleries and boutiques, such as Parlour X (see p085), and some impressive Victorian architecture – stroll down Glenmore Road and take it all in over a drink at The Royal Hotel (No 237, T 9331 2604). In the 1900s, these terrace houses were considered slums, but they are now being snapped up by young, cash-rich urbanites.

CENTRAL BUSINESS DISTRICT

The CBD is not only home to most of Sydney's soaring office towers (see p012) but also its most beautiful parks, and finest art galleries (see p010), restaurants and hotels. Head north and you'll come to Circular Quay on the edge of the harbour (you can catch the Manly Ferry from here; T 131 500), the Opera House (see p014), a revitalised bar and restaurant scene and the historic area known as The Rocks.

LANDMARKS
THE SHAPE OF THE CITY SKYLINE

What do people notice when they walk around Sydney? Locals tend to become a little blind to the beauty that surrounds them, though when the sun hits the sails of the Opera House (see p014) at the right angle, or they spy a grouper fish while snorkelling in Clovelly Bay, they remember their good fortune. Sydney's major landmark, of course, is not actually land: it's the natural haven that is the harbour. From the vast expanse of the South Pacific, the sea flows between North and South Head into many picturesque, secret bays and beaches before forming the Parramatta River.

You can get a good view over the city from the north of the harbour – the upper reaches of Taronga Zoo (Bradleys Head Road, T 9969 2777) are perfect. One oddity you'll notice from here is The Horizon (184 Forbes Street), east of the CBD. No one knows quite what Harry Seidler was thinking when he designed this wavy high-rise block – it would fit in fine among the central skyline, but sticks out like a sore thumb in Darlinghurst. In the middle of the CBD is Sydney Tower (100 Market Street, T 9333 9222), a 309m telecoms facility that locals call Centrepoint. If you have a head for heights, go from the street-level shopping mall to the top and take the Skywalk. On a clear day you can see the Blue Mountains. Those who are braver still should walk up to the apex of the iconic Harbour Bridge; since 1932, the world's tallest steel arch bridge. *For full addresses, see Resources.*

ntemporary
Art

Museum of
Contemporary
Art Australia

MCA

This site was the arrival point of the First Fleet in 1788 (on land which had been home to the Gadigal people for thousands of years) and Australia's original naval dock was constructed here. In 1989, the Museum of Contemporary Art (MCA) moved into the sandstone art deco Maritime Services Building, which was designed in 1939 by WH Withers but delayed by WWII and not finished until 1952. As the MCA collection grew in scope and popularity, the facility was redeveloped and a contemporary wing, designed by Sam Marshall, opened in 2012, at a cost of $53m. Jenga-like blocks in black, white, grey and brown are piled on top of each other and glazed staircases link to the main building, allowing views from each level. There's also a rooftop sculpture garden and café (T 9250 8443). *140 George Street, T 9245 2400, www.mca.com.au*

Aurora Place

Renzo Piano's first Australian project was completed in 2000. The slender, twisted form of Aurora Place stands out as a unique vision among the CBD's forest of uniform office towers, distinctive for the bulge of its east facade and the glass curtain wall that extends independently in a curve beyond the 188m height of the roof. Linked by a glass-covered square that displays artist Kan Yasuda's *Touchstones* sculpture, the building consists of an 18-storey residential block and a separate 41-floor office tower, featuring fins and sails in an ethereal tribute to the Opera House (see p014). Nearby, Lord Foster's 2005 Deutsche Bank (126 Phillip Street), with its stepped upper floors and triangular masts, makes a similarly bold statement on the city's central skyline.
88 Phillip Street, www.auroraplace.com.au

Bondi Beach

On a sunny day, as many as 40,000 people swarm to Australia's most famous stretch of sand. It's certainly not the prettiest beach in Sydney, but as with seemingly everything in this town, it's all about location, location, location. Just 8km from the heart of the city, Bondi is a place for people from all over the world, as well as Sydneysiders. They swim, surf, sunbathe and stroll along the promenade, which runs the kilometre length of the beach. It even boasts its own television programme, *Bondi Rescue*, which premiered in 2006 and follows the days of the local lifeguards, the all-in-blue professionals who patrol the shore year-round. On the beach itself is another Australian icon, the Bondi Surf Bathers' Life Saving Club (T 9300 9279). Formed in 1907, it's the oldest in the world.

Sydney Opera House

After 14 years of controversy, the 'big house' opened its doors with a staging of *War and Peace* in 1973. It is now regarded as one of the world's great contemporary buildings – despite late Danish architect Jørn Utzon leaving the project in 1966 over creative and budgetary disputes. In 1999, Utzon (who never returned to Australia) agreed to help restore his masterpiece. With his son, Jan, and Sydney architect Richard Johnson, he designed a 45m loggia along the west-facing foyers that opened in 2006. There is only one Utzon-designed interior in the entire building – that of the Utzon Room, which boasts an eye-catching tapestry. There are guided tours every half hour, or admire the building's famous silhouette from the terrace bar (see p038). *Bennelong Point, T 9250 7111, www.sydneyoperahouse.com*

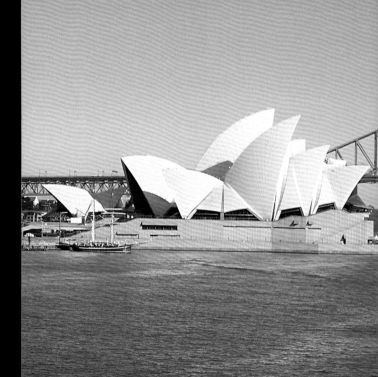

HOTELS

WHERE TO STAY AND WHICH ROOMS TO BOOK

Sydney's harbour location means that visitors eagerly anticipate water views when booking a room. Some of the big city hotels, such as the InterContinental (117 Macquarie Street, T 9253 9000), housed in the former Treasury building, can provide one. As can the revamped Park Hyatt (see p020), perched under the stanchion of the bridge. Its three new rooftop suites are the best and largest in town. Further along the shore is The Sebel Pier One (opposite), whose own renovations do justice to its sparkling location.

However, for a city that prides itself on its beach culture, there are surprisingly few upmarket hotels that take advantage. The pick is Ravesi's (118 Campbell Parade, T 9365 4422), overlooking Bondi, but on the weekends the fallout from the pumping bar downstairs can't be avoided. For privacy in a similar location, design company Robert Plumb lets Bondi 113 (113 O'Donnell Street, T 9316 9066), a chic, airy three-bedroom villa not far from the sand. At Coogee Beach, the homey, relaxed Dive (234 Arden Street, T 9665 5538) has three petite rooms with ocean views.

Perhaps it's best to keep it urban. Kings Cross and Potts Point are perfectly located for business and pleasure. You can walk to the CBD and Darlinghurst (see p039), and some of Sydney's most happening joints are on your doorstep. The Diamant (see p026) is an excellent choice, especially if you can afford the penthouse. *For full addresses and room rates, see Resources.*

The Sebel Pier One

A short walk from The Rocks, this hotel sits in a tranquil waterside spot, close to Sydney's beautiful old wharves, many of which have been converted into arts venues and apartments. In 2011, Sebel gave its rooms an apt nautical overhaul featuring rafters and whitewashed timber ceilings by interior designers Hecker Guthrie. Many benefit from westward harbour views; the Walsh Bay Suite (above) and the Waterside King Suite offer vistas of the Harbour Bridge. Downstairs, there's a relaxed bar and restaurant, and also some good options in Walsh Bay. Try Firefly (T 9241 2031), a waterfront wine bar, or the laidback Cafe Sopra (T 8243 2700), an Italian eaterie where the flavours are as fresh as the sea breeze.
11 Hickson Road, T 8298 9999,
www.sebelpierone.com.au

Fraser Suites
Foster + Partners' 42-floor glass tower
comprises a Manhattan-style all-suite
hotel. Spacious living quarters have
a minimalist design, original art and a
kitchen; we like the One Bedroom Deluxe
Suite (pictured). The airy lobby is all high
ceilings and travertine marble, and the
gym features a 20m cantilevered pool.
488 Kent Street, T 8823 8888,
sydney.frasershospitality.com

Park Hyatt

After an 11-month, A$65m makeover, the Park Hyatt reopened swankier than ever in 2012. Wrapped around the harbour at Campbells Cove, the low-slung, sandstone building is fitting for its Rocks location. There are 155 rooms, such as the Opera Deluxe (above), all with balcony terraces, including three rooftop suites adjacent to the pool deck (opposite): the Sydney is the grandest and has almost 360-degree views. The focus is on 'residential style', with dining tables instead of desks. Spread around the hotel is commissioned work by eight Australian artists, including GW Bot's carved sandstone panels. Have a meal in The Dining Room (T 9256 1661), or stroll to Peter Gilmore's nearby Quay (T 9251 5600), one of Australia's finest restaurants.
7 Hickson Road, T 9256 1234,
www.sydney.park.hyatt.com

Kirketon Hotel

Bought in 2004 by 8Hotels, this is one of the city's most acclaimed boutique establishments. It's still extremely good value, especially considering its location and its 2008 update by local interiors company Edge, which took the slightly masculine design and gave it a more luxe, moody overtone. Gone are the hard edges, replaced instead by modern chandeliers, heavy curtains and leather sofas layered with velvet cushions. The standard rooms are perfect for single travellers, and couples could make themselves very comfortable in one of the Premium or Executive Rooms. Be sure to check out Eau De Vie (T 9357 2470), the speakeasy-inspired cocktail bar situated behind the lobby (above). *229 Darlinghurst Road, T 9332 2011, www.kirketon.com.au*

The Darling

When Sydney's much-maligned casino complex got an extensive nip and tuck in 2011, it reopened with 171 extra rooms, which are located so that you can ignore the poker floor if you desire. The Darling is the first five-star digs to open here since the 2000 Olympics, and it has a vibe that's very now. The lobby (overleaf) is lush and inviting; bibelot-laden shelves beg to be inspected and rugs are by designer Akira Isogawa, although rooms don't quite live up to this promise. We suggest you book a Jewel Suite (above), which has a separate living area and spacious bathroom. Relax at the Asian-inspired Spa and reserve a table at Sokyo, where former Nobu chef Chase Kojima serves contemporary Japanese fare in stunning surrounds.
80 Pyrmont Street, T 9777 9000,
www.thedarling.com.au

Lobby, The Darling

Diamant Hotel

There's a pecking order to the suites at the Diamant, which was opened on a busy intersection in Kings Cross in 2007. Standout rooms include the Penthouse (above), an undeniably chic pied-à-terre designed by Sydney-based firm Burley Katon Halliday. It houses three bedrooms, a spacious open living area and two balconies overlooking the city and harbour, and is perfect for entertaining. The Courtyard Rooms and Suite also have decks with views down William Street, but other rooms don't have outdoor access. However, in keeping with the sleek lobby (opposite), all boast a smart, contemporary design by Edge. There is no restaurant but you are not short of dining options in the area. Indeed, just down the road, Tomislav (T 9356 4535) serves modern Australian fusion in the distinctive Art Wall Building. *14 Kings Cross Road, T 9295 8888, www.8hotels.com*

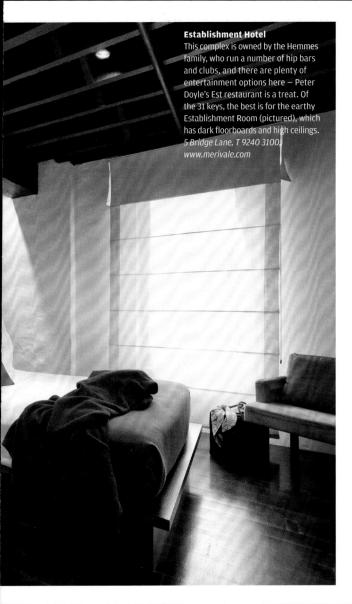

Establishment Hotel

This complex is owned by the Hemmes family, who run a number of hip bars and clubs, and there are plenty of entertainment options here – Peter Doyle's Est restaurant is a treat. Of the 31 keys, the best is for the earthy Establishment Room (pictured), which has dark floorboards and high ceilings.
5 Bridge Lane, T 9240 3100,
www.merivale.com

Blue

Taj Hotels acquired the W Sydney in 2006 and rebranded it as Blue. The 100 rooms, such as the Wharf King (above), are chic and luxurious, if a little small, and the setting – within an old finger wharf at Woolloomooloo, originally built in 1910 during the wheat and wool boom – gives the hotel its unique charm. Lounging on the ottomans and banquettes in the low-lit WaterBar (opposite) is a great way to start or end a night on the tiles. There are plenty of great restaurants located on the waterfront here, including seafood palace Manta (T 9322 3822) and Otto (T 9368 7488), where chef Richard Ptacnik reinterprets modern Italian cuisine. *6 Cowper Wharf Road, T 9331 9000, www.tajhotels.com/sydney*

24 HOURS

SEE THE BEST OF THE CITY IN JUST ONE DAY

Those beaches can be awfully distracting, but if you go home with tan lines and little else you'll have missed many of the aspects that make Sydney one of the most visited cities in the world. Ask a local for their top tips and you're unlikely to hear a consensus, although most ideas are sure to be gems – a beer garden for sundowners, a beach that's great for windsurfing, a restaurant where the food and atmosphere combine for a unique experience. Here we offer you a few of our highlights. Just remember your comfy shoes.

Get up at dawn – really, it is worth it – and have a dip at Bondi Beach (see p013) to shake off the cobwebs before making for The Shop (opposite) for breakfast. There's time now for some culture. Over four floors, the White Rabbit gallery (see p034) shows one of the world's most significant private collections of contemporary Chinese art. Soak in yet more Asian inspiration over lunch at sleek Japanese restaurant Ocean Room (see p036). Take a post-prandial stroll around the Royal Botanic Gardens (see p037) and if you've time, pop by the Art Gallery of New South Wales (Art Gallery Road, T 9225 1744), which, thanks to a revamp in 2012, now houses the most extensive display of modern art in Australia. In the evening, head to Darlinghurst (see p039), where new pint-sized venues seem to open daily, and most do tapas-style sharing plates to fuel your bar hop. There's enough action here to keep you busy all night. *For full addresses, see Resources.*

08.30 The Shop and Wine Bar

The morning food offerings along the beach at Bondi can be overpriced and underwhelming, which is why you should make like a local and head to this hole-in-the-wall café on a side street. There are a couple of tables in the tiny room, lined with retro wallpaper, but a stool under the awning on the footpath is just the place for a sunny start. Of course, there's great coffee, but it's the slightly offbeat variations on favourite dishes – roasted 'shrooms with Persian feta, and BLTs with added gherkins and cheese – that keep people coming back. If you love the vibe, return in the evening, when the place transforms into a wine bar, and order the home-cooked special.
78 Curlewis Street, T 9365 2600

10.00 White Rabbit

Kerr and Judith Neilson have amassed a hugely impressive collection of post-millennium Chinese art. When they ran out of hanging space at home, the couple bought this brick warehouse – a former Rolls-Royce showroom – in inner-city Chippendale and commissioned local architecture firm Smart Design Studio to convert it into a gallery. The Neilsons have acquired painting, sculpture, video and photography by more than 200 artists, mainly emerging talent. The collection includes (opposite; left to right): Liao Chien-Chung's *Transformer Box* and *Garbage Truck*; Madeln Company's *Spread B-041* tapestry; and Jiao Xingtao's *Happily Forgotten*. Downstairs is a spacious café serving dumplings, homemade sweets and Chinese-grown teas, such as lychee, beneath a cloud of antique birdcages.
30 Balfour Street, T 8399 2867,
www.whiterabbitcollection.org

12.30 Ocean Room

Designer Yasumichi Morita's makeover of this Japanese restaurant on Circular Quay in 2010, which included a chandelier installation of 40,000 wooden cylinders hanging from the ceiling, gave it a real wow factor. Chef Raita Noda's menu is just as contemporary and, at times, perhaps a little intimidating. The signature dish is tuna 'wing' and, due to its complexity, comes complete with a map. For the less adventurous, there's superb sushi and sashimi, as well as interesting small plates for sharing. Try the Wagyu beef *harami* charcoal-grilled on a *hida konro*, with miso and spicy sauce. The cocktail list features drinks such as a Wasabi Collins. Lunch is not served at weekends, so instead take a seat at the MCA's rooftop café (see p010). *Overseas Passenger Terminal, T 9252 9585, www.oceanroomsydney.com*

15.00 Royal Botanic Gardens

Australia's oldest scientific institution, founded by Governor Macquarie in 1816, is located in the Domain, the area south of the Opera House. The gardens provide a beautiful environment for an educational amble. Seek out the famous Wollemi Pine, once thought to have been extinct for two millennia, or inspect the tropical flora in one of the two huge greenhouses, one shaped like an arc, the other, a pyramid (above). Maps are available at the Palm Grove Centre. Nearby, the Art Gallery of New South Wales (see p032) contains a large collection of Australian works, including pieces by Aboriginal artists such as Ginger Riley Munduwalawala. It also has a contemporary wing. From here it's a pleasant stroll back down to the shore. *Mrs Macquaries Road, T 9231 8111, www.rbgsyd.nsw.gov.au*

19.30 Opera Bar

By now, you're probably in the market for a cold one. Look for the crowd that gathers on the forecourt below the Opera House and you'll have found the bar. The views of the harbour and city skyline are impressive, and you can't beat snagging a table on the enormous outdoor terrace when the sun is shining. There's also an indoor area with booths, ottomans, high tables and an impressively long bar, which dispenses cocktails such as the Dirty Carpet Disco (chambord, vanilla-infused vodka, strawberry liqueur, apple juice, soda and berries). The kitchen sends out simple, seasonal fare, including antipasti to share, and steaks off the grill. There's live music from 8.30pm on weekdays and 2pm at weekends, from jazz to funk and soul. *Lower Concourse, Sydney Opera House, T 9247 1666, www.operabar.com.au*

23.30 Darlinghurst

Bordered by the bright lights of Kings Cross and laidback Surry Hills, Darlinghurst became the epicentre of Sydney's small-bar scene after a 2007 change in licensing laws made it easier to open living-room-sized spaces. We suggest a crawl. Start at one of the original venues, Pocket (above; T 9380 7002), a former garage that does a neat line in crêpes and cocktails, and features vintage furniture, exposed brick walls and Steve Garrow street murals. Then there's the Wild West-themed Shady Pines Saloon (256 Crown Street), intimate wine bar Love Tilly Devine (T 9326 9297), and retro-cool Hinky Dinks (T 8084 6379). Many of these spots also have decent kitchens. If you're making a proper night of it, head to the gay-friendly part of Oxford Street and pubs/clubs Stonewall (T 9360 1963) and The Colombian (T 9360 2151).

URBAN LIFE

CAFÉS, RESTAURANTS, BARS AND NIGHTCLUBS

A night out in Sydney doesn't take much planning, and there's so much quality and variety that your only worry is peaking too soon. An evening could start with beers in a chilled out bar like Sticky (see p054), fine dining on Greek cuisine at The Apollo (see p048) or molecular wizardry at Bentley (see p059), then cocktails and a dance at shochu bar Tokonoma (see p053), all of which are a stroll away from each other. There has been an explosion of quirky, independent venues, and not just in Darlinghurst (see p039). The CBD scene has improved beyond recognition as laneway bars open: try the whisky den Shirt Bar (7 Sussex Lane, T 8068 8222); speakeasy-style The Baxter Inn (152-156 Clarence Street); retro-kitsch Grandma's Bar (275 Clarence Street, T 9264 3004); or Grasshopper (1 Temperance Lane, T 9947 9025) amid low lighting and 1970s furniture. As popular as ever is the anything-goes Goodgod Small Club (55 Liverpool Street, T 8084 0587), which hosts bands and DJs, and now has a diner, The Dip (T 9283 8792).

Excitement not seen since the city won the Olympic bid greeted the council's 2012 announcement that 10 restaurant-quality food trucks would grace the streets at all hours, with a smartphone app to track them. Eat Art, for example, serves a Japanese and Korean barbecue prepared by the former sous chef at Tetsuya's (529 Kent Street, T 9267 2900), one of Sydney's top foodie destinations. *For full addresses, see Resources.*

Adriano Zumbo

Pâtissier Adriano Zumbo has become a minor celebrity, challenging contestants on the Aussie version of *Masterchef* to create such tricky desserts as his signature V8 cake, which includes eight vanilla layers. People queue down the street outside his Balmain pâtisserie, and now Zumbo has brought his sweet sensations to the revamped Star casino complex. One half of the space is a quirky shop bursting with childlike colours and adult flavours; the other is for dining-in, with a 'dessert train' (above; the sinful sister of the sushi system). Choose from a zumbaron, his version of the macaron, or offerings like Grandma's Soap, a confection of blueberry compote, fresh blueberries, lavender chantilly and almond crème. *Shop 1, Café Court, The Star, 80 Pyrmont Street, www.adrianozumbo.com*

Ms G's
This Kelvin Ho-designed restaurant/bar spread over four floors draws patrons in with its graffiti, rope installation and pink neon. But the contemporary Asian menu by chefs Jowett Yu and Dan Hong is the reason diners return; try the Vietnamese *bánh mì* rolls and a *yuzu* slushie with limoncello and vodka.
155 Victoria Street, T 8313 1000, www.merivale.com

Porteño

A little bit of Argentina arrived in Surry Hills when chefs Elvis Abrahanowicz and Ben Milgate (with sommelier Joe Valore) opened this carnivore's dream. Having started a citywide love affair with tapas at Bodega (T 9212 7766), they've harnessed the gourmet zeitgeist once more. Porteño features an *asador* (fire pit) and *parrilla* (grill) where meat, fish and seafood sizzle enticingly. The eight-hour wood-fired pork,

and fried Brussels sprouts with lentils and mint have become legendary. There is a no-reservations policy for groups of less than five, but waiting for a table with a Thank You For Smoking cocktail (a twist on the Manhattan) and a plate of pulled pork sliders from the bar menu upstairs at Gardel's is a rather pleasant diversion. *358 Cleveland Street, T 8399 1440, www.porteno.com.au*

Spice Temple

In this city basement eaterie, reminiscent of an opium den, chef Neil Perry's take on regional Chinese cuisine draws on the flavours of Sichuan, Hunan and Guangxi. Chilli lovers will be in their element – the Fish Drowned in Heaven (leatherjacket in Sichuan broth) will numb your lips – but there's also plenty for the sensitive palate. *10 Bligh Street, T 8078 1888, www.rockpool.com.au*

The Apollo

Chef Jonathan Barthelmess is known for modern Italian ventures, and restaurateur Sam Christie for launching Thai sensation Longrain (T 9280 2888), but the two have teamed up in Potts Point to highlight their heritage – The Apollo is a paean to the best of Greece. Not that you'd suspect it from the design of the room (weathered concrete, arched windows, marble bar) by architect George Livissianis. The menu favours heritage over flourish: veal and sweetbread meatballs with *avgolemono* (a lemon-egg sauce); wild weed and cheese pie; and meats roasted over a wood fire. Order The Full Greek for the whole table to receive a series of appetisers, the slow-cooked lamb and lemon potatoes, and a dessert like ouzo-marinated watermelon. *44 Macleay Street, T 8354 0888, www.theapollo.com.au*

Mad Cow

Everything about this showcase restaurant in the Ivy Building (see p070) has the potential to create happiness – the zingy yellow accents among a sea of white; the chipper waiters; the unsurpassed people-watching after dark, as the bar outside fills to capacity; and even the eaterie's kooky moniker. Then there is the choice of grilled steaks, including Wagyu, done any way you please. Chef Christopher Whitehead's skills aren't confined to barbecuing beef, though; Mad Cow also offers a range of seafood dishes and a vegetarian option. Like all the venues at the Ivy, it has its detractors, most of whom say it's too expensive, but if you want to experience a truly exuberant atmosphere at dinner, this is *the* place to come.
*330 George Street, T 9240 3000,
www.merivale.com*

North Bondi Italian Food

Splits in the hospitality world are very rarely amicable, but when chefs Robert Marchetti and Maurice Terzini dissolved their partnership, everyone walked away happy. Marchetti kept this trattoria at the north end of Bondi Beach, and little has changed. It's still a case of share and share alike, from plates of roasted meats to calamari, *baccalà* (salted cod) balls and Italian cheeses. There's a low-key vibe and a no-bookings policy, so arrive early or plan a late supper. Terzini, meanwhile, is still overseeing the chic Icebergs Dining Room & Bar (T 9365 9000) at the other end of the beach, designed by architects Lazzarini Pickering, as well as a newer Mediterranean eaterie, Neild Avenue (T 8353 4400) in Rushcutters Bay.
118-120 Ramsgate Avenue, T 9300 4400, www.idrb.com/northbondi

Toko

There are 200,000 matchsticks in Sydney artist Reni Kung's diverting light feature in the wood-panelled bar (opposite) at Toko. Admire it over a cocktail before dining on the izakaya-style menu, either at the communal table, rubbing shoulders with fashionable young things, or at the counter bar, where the *itamae* turn out excellent sushi and sashimi. In 2009, the deeply chic shochu bar/eaterie Tokonoma (T 9357 6100) opened next door, with the same menu and its own Kung sculpture made from 500,000 resin-coated lentils. Try the Ume Rose Sangria cocktail, a blend of white rum, *umeshu* and rosé wine served with blood orange, berries and hibiscus in a teapot for two. The DJ keeps the place buzzing until late with funk and house.
490 Crown Street, T 9357 6100, www.toko.com.au

Sticky

Finding this bar is half the fun. You need to go to the back of the building, down Taggarts Lane, and make a phone call at the door for someone to let you in. Once you've climbed the stairs, find a spot among the vintage furniture, chandeliers and film posters. This is one of Sydney's original small bars and is still going strong thanks to the warm welcome from owner Michael Fantuz (he also runs the Table For 20 eaterie downstairs). There is an Italian slant to the offerings: plates of cured meats and cheese are available to share, and the day's wine selections, chalked up on the board, range from nebbiolo to sangiovese. There's great music too, often live earlier in the evening. Open Wednesday to Saturday from 6pm.
182 Campbell Street, T 041 609 6916, www.tablefor20.blogspot.com

Chiswick

Chef Matt Moran and restaurateur Peter Sullivan's Aria (T 9252 2555) is a temple to fine dining and harbour views, but it's their second venture that attracts the in-crowd for the home-style Australian cuisine. Set within a park-sized garden, Chiswick has a relaxed vibe; we like to snag a spot on the communal bench (above) next to the kitchen at lunchtimes, although the conservatory (overleaf) is charming.

The menu is centred around the garden and a wood-burning oven, and changes with the seasons. Start with sharing plates – the crisp buttermilk chicken is a favourite, or try the snapper ceviche – and for mains, it's hard to beat the roast lamb, reared on the Moran family farm, Green Hills, and delivered ready to carve. *65 Ocean Street, T 8388 8688, www.chiswickrestaurant.com.au*

Conservatory, Chiswick

The Rum Diaries

No prizes for guessing what this operation is all about. There are roughly 90 varieties of rum on offer and a long list of cocktails, including an excellent mojito and a hot buttered rum for when the nights draw in. The fusion tapas menu has headed in a fine-dining direction since the arrival of chef Gerald Touchard and includes rum-soaked barramundi with vanilla and onion purée and celery bulgar, and a dessert of chocolate marquise served with OP rum and allspice chantilly cream. The three candlelit rooms are reminiscent of a 1920s Paris salon, with furniture and fittings from auction houses, and the owners have built a bar from recycled rail sleepers, as well as highly original pieces such as the spiralling standalone booth (above).
288 Bondi Road, T 9300 0440,
www.therumdiaries.com.au

Bentley Restaurant & Bar

Many have been predicting the downfall of molecular gastronomy, but chef Brent Savage's Bentley is not going anywhere. He and sommelier Nick Hildebrandt are a formidable team, creating paired food and wine menus that are innovative and superbly considered. The 2010 renovation, spearheaded by acclaimed Melbourne interior designer Pascale Gomes-McNabb, is the final piece in the jigsaw. It is sleek and moody, and features light fittings that resemble crushed paper and a mesh wall that separates the dining room from the bar. We recommend you sample the eight-course tasting menu, which includes dishes such as Balmain bug (a local cousin of the crayfish) with lamb sweetbread, black bean and coconut curd.

320 Crown Street, T 9332 2344,
www.thebentley.com.au

The Winery

The wine list is serious, but no one in this bar takes themselves seriously. The 1889 former Waterworks is full of mismatched chairs, kitsch artwork, ferns and animal horns. An Enomatic system dispenses more than 50 wines by glass, and 'guest' barrels are shipped from the Mudgee region. The courtyard boasts city views.
285a Crown Street, T 9331 0833,
www.thewinerybygazebo.com.au

INSIDER'S GUIDE

ANNA LUNOE, DJ

Although she's been spending a lot of time in LA, writing and producing, DJ Anna Lunoe is a true Sydneysider, most recently residing in Paddington. 'When I'm at home, I love walking for hours, all the way down to the harbour, past the Opera House and back again via the Kings Cross Food Markets (Fitzroy Gardens) for lunch,' she says. If she has visitors in town she takes them to Argentine eaterie Porteño (see p044): 'You always know dinner is going to be great, and then you can go upstairs to Gardel's for a drink.' For something more low-key, Din Tai Fung (World Square, 644 George Street, T 9264 6010) – famous for its pork *xiao long bao* (dumplings) – is worth the queue. However, she insists on dessert from Gelato Messina (241 Victoria Street, T 8354 1223), or its next-door pâtisserie, Creative Department (243 Victoria Street).

To kick off an evening out, Lunoe likes the laidback vibe of The Commons (32 Burton Street, T 9358 1487). 'It's great for catching up with friends.' Later on, there are two very different clubs where she loves to DJ. The Chinese Laundry (111 Sussex Street, T 8295 9999) is one of Sydney's largest and longest-running venues and puts on international and local DJs. 'Go to dance, not to pose,' she advises. Her other favourite is Goodgod Small Club (see p040). 'There is no place in the world I'd rather be. It's run by friends and I've been throwing parties there since it started, so it kind of feels like mine.' *For full addresses, see Resources.*

ARCHITOUR
A GUIDE TO SYDNEY'S ICONIC BUILDINGS

Although Sydney doesn't have the architectural diversity of London or Berlin, having only been settled a little more than 200 years ago, it does have some gems. Darlinghurst Fire Station (Victoria Street/Darlinghurst Road) is an excellent example of Federation Free Style; designed by Walter Liberty Vernon and completed in 1912, it's still in use today. The first major art deco building in Sydney was BMA House (135 Macquarie Street), its facade embellished with koala sculptures. North of the city, in Castlecrag, are 15 houses, built between 1921 and 1935, designed by US couple Walter Burley Griffin and Marion Mahony Griffin, peers of Frank Lloyd Wright. Further north in Wahroonga, Rose Seidler House (see p068) will delight fans of modernism.

And then there's the contemporary, of course. Even before its construction began in 2012, Frank Gehry's Dr Chau Chak Wing Building (Ultimo Road/Darling Drive) at the University of Technology earned the nickname 'the brown bag' for its paper-like design. It is slated to open in 2014. This is a city that prides itself on its harbour, so any land near the shoreline commands megabucks. Equally, though, community activists want such sites to be reclaimed for public use as recreational and cultural areas. For an overview of the city's architecture and history, take a stroll with SAW (T 040 388 8390, www.sydneyarchitecture.org).
For full addresses, see Resources.

Sydney Theatre

In this 2004 performance space, architect Andrew Andersons impressively marries modern design – in the asymmetrical foyer and the slender balcony that provides glimpses of water over the wharves – to the heritage elements of one of the area's old bond stores; the backstage area abuts a convict-hewn sandstone cliff face. For the audience, there are 896 seats covered in stretch fabric rather than the standard velvet, and the floors are carpeted instead of being bare wood. Andersons' Sydney-based firm, PTW, also designed the theatre's Hickson Road Bistro (T 9250 1990). A stunning red glass screen marks the division between the two spaces. *22 Hickson Road, T 9250 1999, www.sydneytheatre.org.au*

The Bathers' Pavilion

Overlooking Middle Harbour at Balmoral Beach, The Bathers' Pavilion is about 15 minutes' drive from the CBD. Originally opened in 1929, the Spanish Mission-style rendered brick building was designed by council architect Alfred Hale and used as a rather ornamental changing room. In the 1960s, due to a huge decline in the numbers of people using the facilities, it was converted into a restaurant. Reopened in 1999, it was transformed by architect Alex Popov, working with chef Serge Dansereau, to create a stunning, bright, fine-dining restaurant and adjoining café serving French cuisine with a twist. If you have a sunny Sunday afternoon to spare, come for a dip and then enjoy the hospitality. *4 The Esplanade, T 9969 5050, www.batherspavilion.com.au*

Rose Seidler House

Harry Seidler, an émigré from Vienna, is one of Australia's most famous sons, and the home he built for his mother in 1950 is possibly the best-preserved example of modernist architecture in the country. The elevated, cubiform building, with glass walls and timber frames, arranged in a U-shape around a flagged terrace, explores the relationship between indoor and outdoor space. All of the original appliances remain in the kitchen, and other rooms are furnished with pieces by Eames, Saarinen and the like. Part of the Historic Houses Trust, it is located 30km north of the city and overlooks a national park (it is open on Sundays, from 10am to 5pm). Aficionados should also check out the Seidler House (see p102). *71 Clissold Road, Wahroonga, T 9989 8020, www.hht.net.au/museums*

Ivy Building
In 2009, Woods Bagot and interior design firm Hecker Phelan & Guthrie converted two adjoining buildings into 20,000 sq m of 1960s Palm Springs-style hedonism. A series of indoor and outdoor spaces comprise a first-floor foliage-bedecked atrium, boutiques, bars, restaurants, including the Mad Cow grill (see p049), and a rooftop pool-party venue.
320-330 George Street, T 9240 3000

SHOPPING

THE BEST RETAIL THERAPY AND WHAT TO BUY

Never has there been a better time to hit Sydney's stores. Retailers are struggling against online competition and only those boasting unique offerings are still pulling customers through the doors.

Although you may need a map and compass to navigate the Westfield complex (450 George Street, T 8236 9200), reopened after a A$1.2bn makeover, it's worth persevering, for its food court alone. There are more than 250 stores and a host of Oz designers under one roof, including the street fashion and denim label Ksubi (T 8246 9130) and flirty, feminine ready-to-wear at Zimmermann (T 8246 9204). Concept store Cara & Co (T 9226 9999) has a highly covetable selection of global brands and an innovative restaurant.

If you'd prefer to avoid the sharp edges and loud music, try one of the inner-city 'villages'. Crown Street in Darlinghurst is lined with eclectic retail, from Via Alley (see p086) to vintage store Grandma Takes a Trip (No 263, T 9356 3322). And Glenmore Road near the junction of Oxford Street is home to the boutiques of local fashion designers Camilla and Marc (Shop 8, Nos 2-16, T 9331 1133), Willow (No 3a, T 9358 4477) and Kirrily Johnston (No 6, T 9380 7775). At weekends, you can't go wrong with the markets. Try Paddington Bazaar (395 Oxford Street) on Saturdays for local art and craft, or the sprawling Bondi Markets (Campbell Parade) for cutting-edge fashion – Sass & Bide started out here.

For full addresses, see Resources.

Sterling

Part of Gaffa Gallery, an exciting artist-run space housed in a former police station in the CBD, this retail space opened in 2010 and specialises in practical works of art by Australian craftspeople. Glassware and ceramics are displayed in stark, glass fixtures, set against whitewashed walls that juxtapose with the dark timber floors of this heritage building. Original and unusual jewellery is accompanied by paraphernalia that shows the creative process from inception to production. Artisans represented here include Mark Vaarwerk, Melinda Young, Dougal Haslem and Natalia Milosz-Piekarska, although the line-up changes regularly.
281 Clarence Street, T 9283 4273, www.gaffa.com.au

Koskela

In 2012, having grown out of its previous premises, Koskela moved to a gigantic warehouse in the semi-industrial suburb of Rosebery. Furniture designer Russel Koskela has a Scandinavian heritage, and his pieces – all clean, low lines, quality finishes and eco-friendly materials such as recycled hardwoods – suit this raw space. There is also an expanding range of artisanal products, from handprinted bedlinen to sculptural light shades (left, top) created in conjunction with Yolngu weavers from Arnhem Land, and sourced by Koskela's wife, Sasha Titchkosky. In the workshop, visiting craftspeople and artists reveal their methods. There's also an art gallery space in the canteen-style Kitchen By Mike (T 9045 0910), run by the former chef at legendary seafood grill Rockpool (T 9252 1888).
85 Dunning Avenue, T 9280 0999,
www.koskela.com.au

Published Art

You definitely won't be able to buy the new Stephenie Meyer release here, because you won't find anything on the shelves apart from the latest art, film, architecture, fashion, photography and design books, periodicals and magazines. Since 1999, Published Art has been the bookstore that Sydney's creative community returns to again and again for inspiration, because the stock, which is sourced from a huge range of global publishers, can change daily. Pick up such tomes as *The Architecture of Glenn Murcutt* or *70/80/90 Iconic Australian Houses*. Or discuss your interests with owner Sharon Tredinnick, who is usually found behind the counter and commands a wealth of knowledge. *Shop 2, 23-33 Mary Street, T 9280 2839, www.publishedart.com.au*

Assin

In a city that has a reputation for a casual, colourful approach to fashion, the 2008 arrival of a Melbourne retailer renowned for stocking avant-garde international designers including Ann Demeulemeester and Haider Ackermann came as rather a surprise. However, as this store reveals, there's more to Assin's roster, which includes Japanese streetwear from Undercover and Miharayasuhiro, and classic French labels Dior Homme and Lanvin, and it quickly became a must-visit for fashion editors. The venue's visual language is austere, all steel, glass and concrete, pale walls and floors and low-key racking, but it's an interactive experience, which includes a revolving gallery space and video art installations.
12 Verona Street, T 9331 6265,
www.assin.com.au

Victor Churchill

This elegant meat supplier opened in 2009 and is led by father-and-son duo Vic and Anthony Puharich. Designed in collaboration with Michael McCann, it features a flavour-infusing Himalayan salt brick wall and Calacatta floors. Try the dry-aged Black Angus and jamón Ibérico de bellota for a gourmet picnic. *132 Queen Street, T 9328 0402, www.victorchurchill.com*

Planet

Beautifully displayed in this converted garage, with its polished raw concrete floors, bare brick walls and bright red walls, is designer Ross Longmuir's range of contemporary furniture, created using sustainably grown Australian hardwoods, alongside craft and design items by more than 70 artisans. There are one-off ceramics by some of the country's best makers, including Kris Coad, Szilvia Gyorgy and Christopher Plumridge, such as his teabowl (above), A$55, as well as homewares, textiles and lighting. Most of the pieces, chosen for their charm, functionality and integrity, are produced in Australia, but you'll also find hand-loomed rugs from India and recycled vintage fabrics from France and Japan. *114 Commonwealth Street, T 9211 5959, www.planetfurniture.com.au*

Aesop
Designed by Rodney Eggleston of March
Studio and company founder Dennis
Paphitis, the smooth, contemporary
lines of Aesop's slick store are a breath
of fresh air in the historic Strand Arcade.
The full range of plant-based products
is available here. Try the Rosehip Seed
Lip Cream, perfect for the flight home.
Shop 20, 412–414 George Street,
T 9235 2353, www.aesop.net.au

Becker Minty

There's a bit of everything in this Potts Point emporium at the base of the Ikon Building. It carries fashion – including Etiqueta Negra and Campaign for men, and Melinda & Narina and Aurelio Costarella for women – art, ceramics, accessories, aromatherapy products, lighting, stationery and even tasteful trinkets. But you don't have to dig deep to discover something covetable because owners Jason Minty and James Vaile have excellent taste and they source from across the globe. A second branch of Becker Minty opened in 2010 in Woollahra (T 9328 5185) and functions as a gift outlet, ideal for jewellery and home accessories. *Shop 7, Ikon Building, 81 Macleay Street, T 8356 9999, www.beckerminty.com*

Parlour X

The rails at Eva Galambos' enchanting boutique are always hung with highly desirable fashion and accessories; investment pieces from labels such as Jérôme Dreyfuss, Peter Pilotto and Isabel Marant are among the on-trend edit. The store was designed by architect Nick Tobias and features walls of mirrors with an art deco motif, oak herringbone floors, Victorian and Georgian cabinets and contemporary lighting. Upstairs is beauty salon Parlour B (T 9331 0728), where Nathan Williams is the city's eyebrow king. Nearby, visit Land's End (T 9331 2656) for Australian designers Toni Maticevski and Dion Lee, and The Corner Shop on William Street (T 9380 9828), which carries a savvy range of on-the-rise local labels. *213 Glenmore Road, T 9331 0999, www.parlourx.com.au*

Via Alley

You have to admire retailers who, even in tough times, work with designers to create a unique experience. Ben Hsu and Jane Lo's shop sells fashion from Cosmic Wonder and Tsumori Chisato, as well as the limited-edition results of alliances with artists, collectible toys, homewares, cameras and left-field magazines and books, including Via Alley publications.
Shop 3, 285a Crown Street, T 8354 0077

SPORTS AND SPAS

WORK OUT, CHILL OUT OR JUST WATCH

It's no secret that Australians love sport, and Sydney's facilities, enhanced by the city hosting the 2000 Olympics, are second to none. Swimmers are spoilt for choice thanks to plenty of outdoor pools, often created around natural rock formations, including the Andrew 'Boy' Charlton Pool (1c Mrs Macquaries Road, T 9358 6686), Wylie's Baths (Neptune Street, T 9665 2838) and the Bondi Icebergs (1 Notts Avenue, T 9130 3120). In the harbour, Camp Cove near Vaucluse is a great snorkelling spot and not far from beautiful Neilsen Park, with its picnic spots and the neo-Gothic Greycliffe House. Surfers should head to the schools at Bondi and Manly. On land, boot camp is popular with fitness fanatics and often takes place in a picturesque setting – enquire at any gym. Or join the joggers on the route through the Botanic Gardens (see p037) down to the water, and the trail that links Bondi and Bronte.

For those who prefer to spectate, summer means cricket and winter brings rugby league, rugby union and Australian Rules (AFL). In 2012, a second Sydney team, the Greater Western Sydney Giants, joined the AFL fray and play matches at the Škoda Stadium (1 Showground Road) and ANZ Stadium (Edwin Flack Avenue, T 8765 2000). But the local heroes are the Sydney Swans, who play at the Sydney Cricket Ground (Moore Park Road, T 9360 6601), which has a lovely members' pavilion dating from 1886. *For full addresses, see Resources.*

The Observatory Day Spa

If you thought caviar was just for blinis, and that gold, diamonds and pearls were for jewellery, a trip to The Observatory Hotel's day spa will set you straight. Book a 90-minute Pure Gold Radiance Treatment or the exclusive four-and-a-half-hour Observatory Champagne and Caviar Indulgence, which involves a full-body massage followed by a Caviar Firming Facial, using Carita products.

It's topped off with a mani and pedi while you sip on a glass of Duval-Leroy rosé. The excellent facilities here comprise a steam room, a sauna and a 20m indoor pool (above) that sits below an arched ceiling. *89-113 Kent Street, T 8248 5250, www.observatoryhotel.com.au*

Origin
Opened by Wild Life Hair in 2010, this salon boasts jaw-dropping views of the Opera House and the Harbour Bridge, and its Michelle Latham interiors (low cutting stations and Paul Smith fabrics) add to the hip atmosphere. Unwind with a blend of Single Origin coffee and iPads loaded with fashion magazines.
1-20 Alfred Street, T 9955 4990, www.wildlifehair.com

King George V Recreation Centre

This site has been a sports venue since the 1920s, but the recreation centre designed by Lippmann Associates for its 1998 reincarnation is firmly contemporary. Thirty-five-metre curved-steel roof trusses form the internal bones of the building, the eastern facade is transparent and the side that backs on to the expressway leading to Harbour Bridge is painted with a community mural. The centre runs classes in everything from yoga to cardio-boxing, and there are basketball, volleyball, netball and badminton courts; outside are hoops and tennis facilities. But perhaps a better bet for tennis are the courts nestled in a lovely valley in Cooper Park (T 9389 3100), which feel a lot further out of the city than the 15-minute drive from the CBD. *Cumberland Street, T 9244 3600, www.cityofsydney.nsw.gov.au*

Ian Thorpe Aquatic Centre
Designed by Harry Seidler & Associates
and completed in 2007, this centre
is a collaboration between the city
council and the YMCA to provide
community-based fitness facilities.
You'd never know you were at the Y,
though, with its state-of-the-art gym,
three pools, sauna and steam room.
458 Harris Street, T 9518 7220,
www.itac.org.au

ESCAPES

WHERE TO GO IF YOU WANT TO LEAVE TOWN

You'll probably never find yourself bored in Sydney, but if you have the good fortune to spend an extended period of time here, jump in a car and explore further afield. Just to the west are the Blue Mountains (the vapours emitted by the eucalyptus trees give them a faint hue), where a string of quaint villages – Katoomba is the largest, though Blackheath and Leura are also popular – offer antiques shopping, fine dining and exceptional local produce. Drop off the western side of the mountains and you'll find Wolgan Valley Resort (see p098), in an area surrounded by national parks.

North of the city are strings of beaches, including the celebrity favourite, Palm Beach. Hole up with a group of friends at Rockridge (T 9331 2881), a restored 1940s whitewashed villa that overlooks the ocean and is available for rent. Slightly further away are the harbours, inlets and vast stretches of surf and pristine sand that comprise Brisbane Water. Here, by tranquil Hardys Bay, you'll find Pretty Beach House (83 High View Road, T 4360 1933), a retreat with three pavilions, heated plunge pools and superlative cuisine.

Australia's capital, Canberra, is just over three hours' drive away. It doesn't have the energy of Sydney or Melbourne, populated, as it is, mainly by politicians and students. However, it boasts some fantastic city planning and architecture, including Ashton Raggatt McDougall's National Museum of Australia (see p100).

For full addresses, see Resources.

Huski, Falls Creek, Victoria

The ski season in the Australian Alps runs from June to October. The region's Mount Hotham Airport is an 85-minute flight from Sydney, and after a two-hour drive you'll reach the resort of Falls Creek. Huski, designed by Melbourne architects Elenberg Fraser, was inspired by the angles of a snowflake and has 14 rooms, from studios (which have a spa bath instead of a balcony jacuzzi) to huge penthouses, all with sweeping views. If it's booked up, an alternative is the ski-in/ski-out Fjäll (T 03 9650 0509), by architects Salter and interior designers Hecker Phelan & Guthrie, which has a ski-lodge feel. Its six Scandi-style apartments are decked out with wood panelling, midcentury furniture, marble kitchens and hot tubs on the balcony.
3 Sitzmark Street, T 1300 652 260, www.huski.com.au

Wolgan Valley Resort & Spa
This tranquil retreat is set in the Greater
Blue Mountains World Heritage Area,
a vast reserve that is home to kangaroos,
koalas, wallabies, potoroos, bettongs and
96 species of bird, including the rare glossy
black cockatoo. The resort's 40 luxurious
suites – each with a private plunge or lap
pool – are built of sandstone and timber.
2600 Wolgan Road, Wolgan Valley,
T 6350 1800, www.wolganvalley.com

Canberra

The home of Australian politics is the best-designed city in the country. In 1911, an international planning competition was won by Chicago architects Walter Burley Griffin and Marion Mahony Griffin, and construction on the greenfield site began in 1913. The design is based on geometric shapes, and driving around London Circuit, on the north shore of Lake Burley Griffin, wondering which exit to take, is a rite of passage. For art and architecture lovers, there is much of interest: Ashton Raggatt McDougall's National Museum of Australia (above; T 6208 5000); the brutalist High Court (T 6270 6811), designed by Edwards Madigan Torzillo Briggs; the National Portrait Gallery (T 6102 7000) by Johnson Pilton Walker, opened in 2008; and even Embassy Drive. Stay at the Diamant Hotel (T 6175 2222) for its style and location.

Seidler House, Southern Highlands
Designed by the late Harry Seidler (see p068) and finished in 2000, this striking four-bedroom villa perches over a deep gorge in the bush near Bowral, halfway to Canberra. Built into the sandstone, it has a sweeping wave-like roof, floor-to-ceiling glass walls and an outdoor rock pool. 'It's a partnership with nature,' said Seidler. 'It's poetic and beautiful.'
www.contemporaryhotels.com.au

NOTES

SKETCHES AND MEMOS

RESOURCES
CITY GUIDE DIRECTORY

HOTELS
ADDRESSES AND ROOM RATES

Blue 030
Room rates:
double, from A$280;
Wharf King, from A$850
6 Cowper Wharf Road
Woolloomooloo Wharf
T 9331 9000
www.tajhotels.com/sydney

Bondi 113 016
Room rates:
Villa, from A$2,300 per weekend
113 O'Donnell Street
T 9316 9066
www.robertplumb.com.au

The Darling 023
Room rates:
double, from A$270;
Jewel Suite, from A$780
80 Pyrmont Street
T 9777 9000
www.thedarling.com.au

Diamant Hotel Canberra 100
Room rates:
double, from A$200
15 Edinburgh Avenue
Canberra
T 6175 2222
www.8hotels.com

Diamant Hotel Sydney 026
Room rates:
double, from A$175;
Courtyard Room, from A$265;
Courtyard Suite, from A$315;
Penthouse, from A$2,000
14 Kings Cross Road
T 9295 8888
www.8hotels.com

Dive 016
Room rates:
double, from A$165
234 Arden Street
T 9665 5538
www.divehotel.com.au

Establishment Hotel 028
Room rates:
double, A$470;
Establishment Room, A$540
5 Bridge Lane
T 9240 3100
www.merivale.com

Fjäll 097
Room rates:
double, A$1,400
7 Snowgums Lane
Falls Creek
Victoria
T 03 9650 0509
www.fjall.com.au

Fraser Suites 018
Room rates:
double, A$430;
One Bedroom Deluxe Suite, A$490
488 Kent Street
T 8823 8888
sydney.frasershospitality.com

Huski 097
Room rates:
double, from A$175;
Studio, A$175;
Penthouse, A$600
3 Sitzmark Street
Falls Creek
Victoria
T 1300 652 260
www.huski.com.au

InterContinental 016
  Room rates:
  double, from A$275
  117 Macquarie Street
  T 9253 9000
  www.intercontinental.com
Kirketon Hotel 022
  Room rates:
  double, from A$175;
  Premium Room, from A$310;
  Executive Room, from A$385
  229 Darlinghurst Road
  T 9332 2011
  www.kirketon.com.au
Park Hyatt 020
  Room rates:
  double, from A$795;
  Opera Deluxe, A$1,200;
  Sydney Suite, A$16,000 per night
  (two-night minimum stay)
  7 Hickson Road
  T 9256 1234
  www.sydney.park.hyatt.com
Pretty Beach House 096
  Room rates:
  double, from A$1,700
  83 High View Road
  Pretty Beach
  Brisbane Water
  T 4360 1933
  www.prettybeachhouse.com.au
Ravesi's 016
  Room rates:
  double, from A$160
  118 Campbell Parade
  T 9365 4422
  www.ravesis.com.au

Rockridge 096
  Room rates:
  Villa, from A$900
  Palm Beach
  T 9331 2881
  www.contemporaryhotels.com.au
The Sebel Pier One 017
  Room rates:
  double, from A$210;
  Waterside King Suite, from A$800;
  Walsh Bay Suite, from A$1,000
  11 Hickson Road
  T 8298 9999
  www.sebelpierone.com.au
Seidler House 102
  Room rates:
  House, from A$1,500 per night
  (two-night minimum stay)
  Wingecarribee River
  Bowral
  Southern Highlands
  T 9331 2881
  www.contemporaryhotels.com.au
Wolgan Valley Resort & Spa 098
  Room rates:
  Suite, from A$1,950
  2600 Wolgan Road
  Wolgan Valley
  T 6350 1800
  www.wolganvalley.com

WALLPAPER* CITY GUIDES

Executive Editor
Rachael Moloney

Editor
Jeremy Case
Author
Carrie Hutchinson

Art Director
Loran Stosskopf
Art Editor
Eriko Shimazaki
Designer
Mayumi Hashimoto
Map Illustrator
Russell Bell

Photography Editor
Sophie Corben
Acting Photography Editor
Elisa Merlo
Photography Assistant
Nabil Butt

Chief Sub-Editor
Nick Mee
Sub-Editor
Marie Cleland Knowles

Editorial Assistant
Emma Harrison

Interns
Carmen de Baets
Despina Rangou

**Wallpaper* Group
Editor-in-Chief**
Tony Chambers
Publishing Director
Gord Ray
Managing Editor
Jessica Diamond
Acting Managing Editor
Oliver Adamson

Wallpaper* ® is a
registered trademark
of IPC Media Limited

First published 2006
Second edition (revised
and updated) 2010
Third edition (revised
and updated) 2011
Fourth edition (revised
and updated) 2012
Reprinted 2013

All prices are correct at
the time of going to press,
but are subject to change.

Printed in China

PHAIDON

Phaidon Press Limited
Regent's Wharf
All Saints Street
London N1 9PA

Phaidon Press Inc
180 Varick Street
New York, NY 10014

Phaidon® is a registered
trademark of Phaidon
Press Limited

www.phaidon.com

ISBN 978 0 7148 6639 0

PHOTOGRAPHERS

Peter Bennetts
Fraser Suites,
pp018-019
Kirketon Hotel, p022
Diamant Hotel, p026, p027
The Shop and
Wine Bar, p033
Sticky, p054
The Rum Diaries, p058
The Winery, pp060-061
Published Art, p076
Becker Minty, p084
Via Alley, pp086-087
Huski, p097

Brett Boardman
MCA, pp010-011
Park Hyatt, p020, p021
The Darling, p023,
pp024-025
Pocket, p039
Adriano Zumbo, p041
Porteño, p044, p045
The Apollo, p048
Chiswick, p055, pp056-057
Anna Lunoe, p063
The Bathers'
Pavilion, pp066-067
Koskela, pp074-075
Parlour X, p085

Richard Bryant
Rose Seidler
House, pp068-069

**Hamilton Lund/
Destination NSW**
Sydney city view,
inside front cover

Ross Honeysett
Aurora Place, p012

Trevor Mein
Ivy Building, pp070-071

Ken Middleton
Bondi Beach, p013
Royal Botanic
Gardens, p037

Paris Neilson
White Rabbit, pp034-035

Nicky Ryan
Toko, p052, p053

George Serras
National Museum of
Australia, pp100-101

**www.thomas
jacobsen.com**
North Bondi Italian
Food, pp050-051

**Jann Tuxford/
Tourism NSW**
Sydney Opera
House, pp014-015

Michelle Young
Ms G's, pp042-043
Bentley Restaurant
& Bar, p059
Sterling, p073
Victor Churchill,
pp078-079
Origin, pp090-091

SYDNEY
A COLOUR-CODED GUIDE TO THE CITY'S HOT 'HOODS

BONDI
The place for beach babes and bars – the surf's better elsewhere, but Bondi's unmissable

DARLINGHURST/SURRY HILLS
This is probably the best part of town for a temporary base, in the heart of boho land

WATERLOO
Squeezed out of Surry Hills by high rents, shops are now opening in this suburban area

POTTS POINT/KINGS CROSS
The sleaze is more sanitised in KC these days but Potts Point remains far more laidback

PADDINGTON
Long since gentrified, this district is now the scene of some truly spectacular shopping

CENTRAL BUSINESS DISTRICT
Unusually, Sydney's financial district is full of beautiful parks, galleries and restaurants

For a full description of each neighbourhood, see the Introduction.
Featured venues are colour-coded, according to the district in which they are located.